IN GOD WE TRUST

A Personal Call to Prayer

Dear Friend,

Wrapped in possibilities, the year 2002 waits on your doorstep ready to be discovered a day at a time. Some discoveries will be wonderful, some challenging. All are sifted through your Savior's loving hand.

The purpose of this journal is for you to capture those important discoveries of your life—the ones that would slip by you if you didn't ponder them a while. To see God's hand both in the details and the broad strokes of your life. To renew your trust in Him—to commit your life to Him each time you write out your prayer to your Father.

But that doesn't happen automatically. Some days you'll sit down to write and can't think of anything to say. Other times your pen will barely keep up with your heart. Both occasions are important because each time you open this prayer journal you say, "Here I am, Lord." Anticipate that time lingering in His presence. In the quietness of those moments before His throne of grace, you'll find what you need—refreshment, perspective, conviction, strength.

My hope is that through the coming year, the title on the front of this journal, *"In God We Trust,"* will become less of a motto on the coins in your pocket and more of a banner that's draped across your life.

May your heart be strengthened and warmed as you draw into a deeper, more intimate relationship with the Lord Jesus. I know you can anticipate some great discoveries ahead!

In God We Trust—

Chuck Swindoll

IN GOD WE TRUST

A Personal Call to Prayer

THIS JOURNAL RECORDS THE PERSONAL CONVERSATIONS BETWEEN GOD AND

____

YOUR NAME

HOLDING THE MEDITATIONS, SIMPLE WONDERS, AND COMMITMENTS OF TRUST DISCOVERED IN THE DAYS OF 2002.

Let me hear Your lovingkindness in the morning;
For I trust in You;
Teach me the way in which I should walk;
For to You I lift up my soul.
Psalm 143:8

THIS NEW YEAR WILL BE LIKE NONE OTHER IN OUR LIVES. EVEN THOUGH WE ARE SURE TO FACE UNEXPECTED TESTS, OUR GOD WILL PROVE HIMSELF FAITHFUL. BY HIS GRACE, WE WILL LEARN AND GROW AND MATURE AS NEVER BEFORE. RENEW YOUR COMMITMENT TO HIS TRUTHS DAILY, REMAIN OPEN TO THE PATH HE DIRECTS, AND TRUST HIM FOR WISDOM IN EACH STEP.

Chuck Swindoll

Week of December 30 through January 5

Weekly Reflection

Just as Abraham "went out, not knowing where he was going" (Hebrews 11:8), we are headed into the unknown future. This year, God will do things in your life that He's never done before. On the road ahead, renew your commitment to trust Him daily. Chuck

Week of January 6 through January 12

Weekly Reflection

I am convinced that by advancing on our knees through every detail of our lives, we will see one obstacle after another removed, one need after another met, one opportunity after another fulfilled. Chuck

Week of January 13 through January 19

Weekly Reflection

Be anxious for nothing, but in everything by prayer and supplication with thanksgiving let your requests be made known to God. (Philippians 4:6)

Week of January 20 through January 26

Weekly Reflection

Whatever circumstance you've written off, that's out of the question, that's impossible—see it from God's perspective. You have a divinely powerful weapon in prayer, when you turn your attitude, your habit, your circumstance over to Him. He'll take charge. Live freely as you rest and abide in God's intervention. Chuck

NOTHING IS HAPPENING ON EARTH THAT BRINGS A SURPRISE TO HEAVEN. NOTHING TOUCHES US THAT HAS NOT FIRST PASSED THROUGH THE FINGERS OF HIS HANDS. THINGS THAT SEEM ALTOGETHER CONFUSING, WITHOUT REASON, UNFAIR, OR EVEN WRONG DO INDEED FIT INTO THE FATHER'S PROVIDENTIAL PLAN.

Chuck Swindoll

Week of January 27 through February 2

Weekly Reflection

God's unique plan includes sudden, unexplainable moves, illogical events, unpredictable changes, and even a few uncomfortable adjustments, but so goes life on the frontier of faith.

Chuck

Week of February 3 through February 9

Weekly Reflection

In the morning, O Lord, You will hear my voice,

In the morning I will order my prayer to You . . . (Psalm 5:3)

Week of February 10 through February 16

Weekly Reflection

Pack five items in your suitcase for your trek across this new year: the desire to obey God, the willingness to be still, a faithfulness to commitments, an eternal perspective, and faith for the unknown. Chuck

Week of February 17 through February 23

May you have:

the mercy of God to forgive you of whatever may block your relationship.

the strength of God to make you resolute to do His will.

the grace of God to be kind, tender, and affectionate to one another.

the patience of God to believe as you wait on Him.

faith in God that He will provide whatever you will need.

the peace of God in whose name all peace resides. Chuck

"Joy is the flag that flies over the castle of the heart, announcing that the King is in residence today." When God reigns in our hearts, His presence is reflected in our response to life's challenges. Trust God today and let His flag fly high!

Week of February 24 through March 2

Weekly Reflection

Devote yourselves to prayer, keeping alert in it with an attitude of thanksgiving. (Colossians 4:2)

Week of March 3 through March 9

Weekly Reflection

It isn't easy to trust God in times of adversity. Feelings of distress, despair, and darkness trouble our souls as we wonder if God truly cares about our plight. But not to trust Him is to doubt His sovereignty and to question His goodness.

Chuck

Week of March 10 through March 16

Weekly Reflection

How is it possible for those who don't know the future to walk into it with faith and courage? That takes insight . . . a balanced blend of wisdom, vision, discernment, intuition, and anticipation. Chuck

Week of March 17 through March 23

Rejoice always; pray without ceasing; in everything give thanks; for this is God's will for you in Christ Jesus. (1 Thessalonians 5:16–18)

Week of March 24 through March 30

Weekly Reflection

In order to trust God we must view our adverse circumstances through eyes of faith, not our senses. And just as the faith of salvation comes through hearing the message of the Gospel (Romans 10:17), so the faith to trust God in adversity comes through the Word of God alone.

Chuck

MAY GOD GIVE US EYES TO SEE THROUGH OUR CIRCUMSTANCES AND TO HEAR HIS VOICE OF REASSURANCE THROUGH THE CRACKS AND CREVICES ALONG THIS JOURNEY CALLED LIFE. AS WE SEEK HIM THIS DAY, MAY NEW INSIGHTS BRING FRESH ENCOURAGEMENT, NEW SOUNDS, AND LONG OVERDUE JOY.

Chuck Swindoll

Week of March 31 through April 6

Weekly Reflection

How often do you meet someone with a frown—one that's bent out of shape—given to grumbling or a bad attitude? What a joy it is to meet those who are not just living like a drudgery through life; they're joyful. Know the difference? The joyful person has chosen to trust God!

Chuck

Week of April 7 through April 13

Weekly Reflection

For we walk by faith, not by sight . . . (2 Corinthians 5:7)

Week of April 14 through April 20

Weekly Reflection

It is only in the Scriptures that we find an adequate view of God's relationship to and involvement in our painful circumstances. It is only through the Scripture, applied to our hearts by the Holy Spirit, that we receive the grace to trust God in everything.

Chuck

Week of April 21 through April 27

Weekly Reflection

We cannot live on yesterday's provision, though hindsight assures us that God will provide. Nor do we have the foresight to know all the details ahead of time. Only He knows those things, and our trust in Him is firm.

Chuck

Week of April 28 through May 4

Weekly Reflection

Be strong and take heart,

all you who hope in the Lord. (Psalm 31:24 NIV)

HOPE FOR OUR GREAT NATION RESTS UPON THE INTEGRITY OF THE INDIVIDUAL. SPIRITUAL MATURITY AND POWER CANNOT BE LEGISLATED BY CONGRESS—THEY ARE SPAWNED IN THE HEART AND CULTIVATED IN THE HOME BEFORE THEY ARE BRED IN THE LAND. THE STRENGTH OF OUR NATION BEGINS WITH YOU.

Chuck Swindoll

Week of May 5 through May 11

Weekly Reflection

Let the words of my mouth and the meditation of my heart

Be acceptable in Your sight,

O Lord, my rock and my Redeemer. (Psalm 19:14)

Week of May 12 through May 18

Weekly Reflection

Most of us have great hindsight. Looking back, life becomes clear, uncomplicated, easy to explain. Who can't see things clearly once they have already occurred? Our greatest resource for facing the unknown without fear or frustration comes from knowing and trusting God.

Chuck

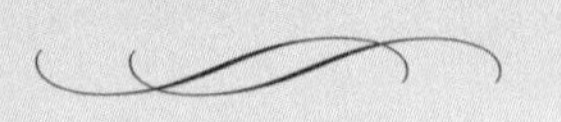

Week of May 19 through May 25

So then, just as you received Christ Jesus as Lord, continue to live in him, rooted and built up in him, strengthened in the faith as you were taught, and overflowing with thankfulness. (Colossians 2:6–7 NIV)

Week of May 26 through June 1

Weekly Reflection

Prayer isn't for God's benefit. He's omniscient! Prayer is for our benefit! He specializes in the things that bruise us, the things for which we would normally worry. Prayer is for you.

Chuck

Acknowledging our dependence on God is critical to godly living. That's what prayer is, you know—our declaration of dependence on God. Prayer says, "We need you Lord . . . desperately."

Chuck Swindoll

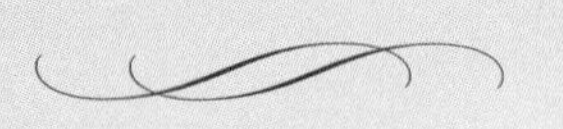

Week of June 2 through June 8

Weekly Reflection

What do you need to entrust to Him? Close to a decision you need to make, a step you need to take, a sin you need to forsake, a choice you need to determine? So, do so today, but talk it over with your Father first. Before the sun sets and tomorrow's demands eclipse today's desires, meet with Him here. Chuck

Week of June 9 through June 15

He who gives attention to the word will find good,

And blessed is he who trusts in the Lord. (Proverbs 16:20)

Week of June 16 through June 22

Weekly Reflection

Developing faith is neither accidental nor incidental. By deliberately focusing on who God is, envisioning what He wants to accomplish, and drawing upon His power to make it happen, we gain the wisdom needed to face the unknown without frustration or fear. Chuck

Week of June 23 through June 29

Weekly Reflection

It helps me to remember that I am not in charge of my day . . . God is. And while I'm sure He wants you to use your time wisely, He is more concerned with the development of your character and the cultivation of the qualities that make you Christlike within. Chuck

God wants your arms around Him. God wants to hear us say, "I love you, Father. I trust You. Whatever You want to give me I accept. I need You. I cling to You. I walk with You. I adore You." God wants your unreserved love, your unqualified devotion, your undaunted trust.

Chuck Swindoll

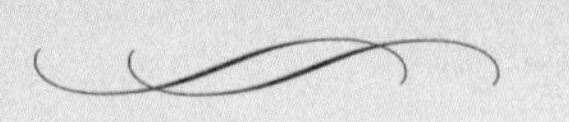

Week of June 30 through July 6

Weekly Reflection

To You, O Lord, I lift up my soul.

O my God, in You I trust . . . (Psalm 25:1–2)

Week of July 7 through July 13

Weekly Reflection

Let us hold fast the confession of our hope without wavering, for He who promised is faithful.

(Hebrews 10:23)

Week of July 14 through July 20

Weekly Reflection

Think about the events and interactions of your day, whether before you or behind you. How would this day look different if you trusted God more?

Chuck

Week of July 21 through July 27

Weekly Reflection

If we are faithless, He remains faithful, for He cannot deny Himself. (2 Timothy 2:13)

GOD IS SOVEREIGN. HE IS IN FULL CONTROL, ORCHESTRATING EVERY DETAIL AND SUSTAINING US NOT ONLY MONTH TO MONTH BUT ON A MOMENT-TO-MOMENT BASIS. WHAT A WONDERFUL CONFIDENCE THERE IS IN KNOWING THAT YOUR GOD IS NOT ONE WHO MERELY SHOWS UP ON THE CHAOTIC SCENES OF YOUR LIFE, BUT ONE WHO KNOWS THE BEGINNING FROM THE END.

Chuck Swindoll

Week of July 28 through August 3

God will stop at nothing to teach you to rely on Him and not the flesh, to turn your attention to Him in humility and dependence. He knows exactly what to strip away so that you are like a piece of clay in His hands. His will is to mold you into a beautiful vessel.

Chuck

Week of August 4 through August 10

View every gift from God as a direct result of His faithful provision for your needs. Once we accept the foundational fact that God owns it all, it is amazing how quickly our priorities fall into place. Chuck

Week of August 11 through August 17

"Be strong and courageous! Do not tremble or be dismayed, for the Lord your God is with you wherever you go." (Joshua 1:9)

Week of August 18 through August 24

Don't be afraid of the lonely times. They can be the best time for your faith to grow. Solitude makes you think deeply. As my mother used to say, "The roots grow deep when the winds are strong." Chuck

Week of August 25 through August 31

The command to "trust in the Lord" is no half-hearted hope of a reluctant heart. On the contrary, it is a conscious acknowledgment of Him "in all your ways." Chuck

Through storm or through calm, God will faithfully provide for our needs. He will calm our storms. He will take care of our families. He will provide what's necessary. And in return, He asks for our trust.

Week of September 1 through September 7

Weekly Reflection

Glory in His holy name;

Let the heart of those who seek the Lord be glad. (Psalm 105:3)

Week of September 8 through September 14

Weekly Reflection

When you willingly give God your trust, nothing becomes more significant than pleasing Him. Entrust your future, family, work, and heart's desire to His safe, loving hand.

Chuck

Week of September 15 through September 21

Weekly Reflection

We are His sheep. When we hear His voice, we follow His leading and trust in Him instead of leaning on our own understanding. He watches over us because we're in His flock: "We are His people and the sheep of His pasture" (Psalm 100:3).

Chuck

Week of September 22 through September 28

Weekly Reflection

When I am afraid,

I will put my trust in You.

In God, whose word I praise,

In God I have put my trust;

I shall not be afraid.

What can mere man do to me? (Psalm 56:3–4)

Week of September 29 through October 5

Weekly Reflection

In silence, His Spirit blends somehow with our inner being. And deep within that mix, as we are before Him and waiting on Him and listening to Him, He connects and gives us a peace—or a lack of peace—according to His will. Chuck

In an impersonal world where we feel more like a number than a person, it is easy to believe that our relationship with God is much the same. Not so. God's Word assures us that our lives have reason and purpose. Let us live today with that comforting confidence . . . God knows what He is about.

Week of October 6 through October 12

Weekly Reflection

Sometimes all we can pray is "Lord, You're the Lord of this. You know that this is a situation that I can't handle. Please, Lord, act. Reveal Your will. Guide me." When you express your dependence, God will show Himself faithful. I've experienced it more times than I can count.

Trust Him. *Chuck*

Week of October 13 through October 19

Weekly Reflection

For our heart rejoices in Him,

Because we trust in His holy name. (Psalm 33:21)

Week of October 20 through October 26

Weekly Reflection

Sometimes worship is an enthusiastic praise of God's majesty. Other times, it's a quiet surrender to His will. A soul at rest in God's character—this, too, is worship. Chuck

Week of October 27 through November 2

Weekly Reflection

Reflect back over the months that are now mere memories. Have there been any significant changes? How about growth? Maybe you've been forced to trust in the Lord in order to stop leaning on your own understanding. Hasn't God been good? Aren't you grateful that He has stayed by your side? Chuck

One of the marks of spiritual maturity is the quiet confidence that God is in control—without the need to understand why He does what He does. He has not forgotten you. He has inscribed your name upon His hand . . . and heart.

Chuck Swindoll

Week of November 3 through November 9

But as for me, I trust in You, O Lord,

I say, "You are my God."

My times are in Your hand . . . (Psalm 31:14–15)

Week of November 10 through November 16

Weekly Reflection

I'm finally learning that His sovereign plan is the best plan. When I keep my hands out of things, His will is accomplished, His name is exalted, and His glory is magnified.

Chuck

Week of November 17 through November 23

Weekly Reflection

For all of you who are doing the right thing day in and day out, yet aren't receiving any praise— take heart! God's eternal rewards include a recognition of faithfulness . . . which is another way of saying, "First the cross, then the crown." Chuck

Week of November 24 through November 30

Offer the sacrifices of righteousness,

And trust in the Lord. (Psalm 4:5)

If finding God's way in the suddenness of storms makes our faith grow broad, then trusting God's wisdom in the "daily-ness" of living makes it grow deep. And strong. What are you trusting God for today?